SHAKESPEARE

AND

ASTROLOGY

From a Student's Point of View

By

WILLIAM WILSON

BOSTON
OCCULT PUBLISHING CO.
204 Dartmouth St.

1903

SHAKESPEARE AND ASTROLOGY.*

If the prognostications of the Science of Planetary Influence as to its own future are to be considered worthy of attention, we may regard ourselves as living on the eve of an interesting era at the present time. Whether Astrology and its presages
be or be not adapted to the use of intelligent people is a question on which even they agree to differ ; we all have what Arte-
mus Ward used to call our idiot syncrasies ; many there are who
hold that the question never attained the dignity of being one ;
probably the position of those alone is safe who have learned to
reserve their judgment until that which forms the basis of so
much adverse criticism is removed, namely, a lack of acquaintance with the subject.

Of one thing we on this planet may rest assured ; if the
fortress of our reason is not yet ready to capitulate to anything
that comes with such queer credentials, there is at least considerable knocking at the gate going on at present. The signs indeed are plentiful that this aged, once esteemed, now jeered at
science occupies not only wider ground today than it has yet
done in our modern life, but that public interest in it is rapidly
on the increase. Astronomers are kept busy preparing Ephemer-
ides of the Planets' Places from year to year ; there are well established publications of the kind ; public library authorities see
fit, not only to inlay their vestibules with the Zodiacal Signs,
but also to include a considerable amount of the literature on
the subject in their lists ; teachers, more or less qualified, there
are in plenty ; serious students abound : in short, it would seem
that Astrology is now ready for that vigorous opposition and
misrepresentation which is always at hand when a great question is ripening for consideration.

As far as its message is concerned, we that have free souls
it touches us not : our withers are not in danger ; we need not
hesitate to hear it, tersely expressed as it has been by a recent
writer. "During the coming century," says this gentleman,
"while the Sun, in the greater cycle, progresses through the
Zodiacal Sign Aquarius, Astrology is destined to become the religion of our race." The prognostication is at least sufficiently

*Copyright 1903 by William Wilson.

distinct, whatever else may be said about it. In olden times the Oracles were careful ; they spoke in generalities ; we of today have changed all that.

Yet the fact remains that Astrology is pressing itself upon the world and is practically demanding to be examined. A religion it may or may not be ; meanwhile, however it comes with an explanation of much that we see in the conduct of the universe which, to most of us, is new ; we hear the word "Science" gravely used in connection with a mysterious something which we have hitherto held to be no more definable and trustworthy than Gypsy (that is, Egyptian) fortune-telling ; and our first feeling is a very curious one. It almost amounts to scare. We are tempted to peep into the temple, the outer doors of which are open, for something says there is a truth, away far back, within. At the same time we are uncomfortably conscious that, by so doing, we subject ourselves to the ridicule of the multitude outside, of our friends, and possibly even of ourselves, if we should emerge from this novel condition of seeing as we never saw before. We therefore fall back on the healthy instinct of our childhood, when we were first confronted with things that touched us strangely, and seek to find out what our fathers thought about them.

As a contribution to this harmless entertainment, it will not be unprofitable to listen to one whose identity may be doubtful, but of whose importance there never has been a question, the writer of the plays of Shakespeare. Of the usefulness of a Science which has played such an enormous part in the history of the world, which had made its mark on nations long before Ptolemy existed, and of which, in their time, men of the acuteness of Addison and Swift thought it well to make so many exhibitions of their ignorance, nothing need be said. The purpose of this paper is attained if it be established that the great English playwright not only was interested in Zodiacal and Planetary questions, but seemed to have found time, at a period when study must have been hampered by the absence of astronomic material, to devote a very considerable portion of his attention to the gaining of knowledge on the subject. The main objection to the enquiry may be at once conceded ; it increases the already large amount of irresponsible talk about him ; but the evil ceases there ; the disintegrating influence of the planets, if it be a factor on earth at all, is as powerful on books and pamphlets as it is on human beings, everything must sooner or later succumb to it ; as for the right or wrong of spending time in such a way, there is nothing good or bad but thinking makes it so. We may know as little of the matter as the philanthropist does of the working classes and yet admit that there is more in heaven and earth than is dreamt of in our philosophy. Shakespeare was a poet, and poetry makes its impress by reason of an occult something that lies behind it ; but the great poets are not content to trust to inspirations ; they busy themselves as well with what is going on around them ; and those are well equipped indeed who have nothing to learn from carefully observing the directions in which their study tends to move.

That there was abundant public interest in Shakespeare's time in the subject of the so-called stargazing. to which so many references are found in the poets of the period, Spencer, Chaucer, Milton, as well as the minor writers, is evident in the third scene of the 5th Act of "Lear," where the aged king comments on the habit of the day. "We take upon us" he says, "the mystery of things, as if we were God's spies. And we wear out in a wall'd prison pacts and sects of great ones that ebb and flow by the moon." In Act 1, Sc. 2, however, Gloster is made to insist that these "late eclipses in the sun and moon portend no good to us." Shakespeare, never didactic, gives to Edmund the following pregnant answer :—

"This is the excellent foppery of the world, that, when we are sick in fortune (often the surfeit of our own behavior) we make guilty of our disasters the sun, the moon and stars ; as if we were villains by necessity, fools by heavenly compulsion, knaves, thieves and treachers by spherical predominance, drunkards, liars and adulterers by an enforced obedience of planetary influence, and all that we are evil in by a divine thrusting on ; an admirable evasion of a man to lay his goatish disposition to the charge of a star. "

Then comes an illustration of a Nativity which would seem to have been frequent in the poet's time, and he closes with what, no doubt, was a sentiment that often found its way into the daily conversation of those about him:—

"Edmund. I am thinking, brother, of a prediction I read
the other day what should follow these eclipses.
Edgar. Do you busy yourself with that ?
Edmund. I promise you the effects he writes of succeed
unhappily. "

Here it is the author himself who is "sectary astronomical"

and concerned with the development of a character under certain well known astrological conditions. This habit of working with Zodiacal types appeared to grow as years went on. There is a beautiful instance of it in one of his later plays. In the 2nd. Scene of the 1st. Act of "Twelfth Night" Sir Toby says, in reply to Andrew's expressed yearning to "set about some revels ;"—

> "What else shall we do? Were we not born under Taurus?
>
> *Sir And.* Taurus? That's sides and heart.
>
> *Sir Toby.* No, sir, it's legs and thighs."

To the uninformed reader such words are meaningless. Singer explains them by saying that the errors were probably intentional ; but Andrew's clearly was not, while Toby's as surely was ; the truth being that Shakespeare, himself a Taurus man, was treating at the time the very best of his Taurian characters (Falstaff and Bottom not forgotten) ; and Toby was not the man to let his friend Capricorn's misstatement pass without rallying him with another. Why he chose that particular one is apparent from the context. Toby had the characteristic Taurian interest in physique, legs had special fascination for him (witness, in a later scene, his remarks on these essentials in the personality of Viola) ; Andrew's shanks in particular took his fancy :—

> "I did think" says he, "by the excellent constitution of thy leg that it was formed under the star of a galliard."
>
> "Aye" says Andrew succumbing to the flattery, " 'tis strong and it does indifferent well in a flame coloured stock."
>
> "What is thy excellence in a galliard, knight?" asks Toby, the exquisite, the inimitable.
>
> "Faith" says the victim, "I can cut a caper." And one can hear the Taurian chuckle and the basso comment, *sotto voce* :—"And I can cut the mutton to't."

In the letter to Malvolio, in the composition of which Toby must have had a hand, (Act 2, Sc. 5) we have the words :—

> "In my stars I am above thee ;
> but be not afraid of greatness."

where the reference clearly is to Jupiter near Midheaven in the tenth or eleventh "house" as opposed to Jupiter beneath the earth at time of birth. This is shown by the subsequent—

"Jove and my stars be praised; Jove, I thank thee; I
will smile, I will do everything that thou wilt have me;"
wherein is expressed the delight of the oppressed Saturnian at
finding himself in the Benefic's favour after all; he will even
forego the one privilege that was afforded him at birth, his rue-
ful countenance; there is to be no holding back; "up to this,"
he says, "I had thought your gracious benefits rather grudg-
ingly bestowed, but there is no mistake about it now, here is
munificence indeed; abject slavery is the very least that can be
offered in return; do with me what you will." That Shakespeare was aware of the qualities attributed to Jupiter is evident
from this, as well as from Act 3, Sc. 1, where Viola says to the
Clown :—"Hold, here's expenses for thee." an, astrologically
speaking, eminently Jovial impulse which elicits the response :—
"Now Jove, in his next commodity of hair, send thee a beard,"
from the observant Clown, who knew he was dealing with
a Jupiterian and recognised the influence of the planet in
her behaviour. The successor to that admirable Viola (and
Sagittarian) Miss Ellen Terry will therefore (if Astrology's prediction about itself be true) not require to be informed that Shakespeare saw his Viola with blonde or light brown hair, she being
a Sagittarian, not only in her relations to others, but in her own
career throughout the play. No one who has interested himself
in this phase of the subject can fail to be impressed with the
grasp of it possessed by Shakespeare. There is scarcely an
utterance in the play that is not significant.

As an illustration of the consistent way in which he worked,
it is worthy of note that Viola's twin has similar characteris-
tics; he also is under the Lord of Sagittarius, although he says,
in Act 2, Sc. 1:

"My stars shine darkly o'er me. Myself and
sister both born in an hour. If the heavens
had been pleased, would we had so ended."

This however was a passing shadow; the fortunate Sagittarian is maintained throughout the comedy; neither suffers want
at any time; even the shipwrecked Viola is treated with consistent poetic license, and seems to have preserved, not only her
presence of mind, but her gold as well, at a time when the loss
of both would have been excusable. As for the brother, her
twin, whose career is similar to her own, he also is within the
text book limits; for, so soon as he meets a danger, in the form
of a tussle with the fighter *par excellence*, Sir Toby Taurus, a

planetary confederate appears and rescues him. Viola, it will be remembered, has also an experience of the kind. It is difficult to imagine that anyone possessed of the most rudimentary acquaintance with the subject could fail to enjoy here the attractive combination of art and science. To suppose it the result of chance would surely involve an effort out of proportion to the necessities of the case. Happy go-luckyism may be a genial guide at times, but sooner or later it sends its victim sprawling. It is easier to suppose that Shakespeare accepted the theory of Zodiacal Influence, and set himself to portray the various types accordingly; as Masson has said, whatever he can be found to have done there is considerable likelihood that he knew he was doing.

Nor, when treating the larger, does he neglect the smaller planets. We have in the 4th. Scene of Act I, the clown saying:–

' Now Mercury endow thee with leasing (lying).''
an instance as significant as that of the Mercury, badly aspected, in "Winter's Tale", our disreputable friend Autolycus ;

"Who, being as I am, littered under Mercury, was
likewise a snapper up of ill-considered trifles,''
a subtle definition when the derivation of the word "consider" is borne in mind. There, of course, is no suggestion here of the Argonaut precursor of this Autolycus ; but, if there were, it would only affect the range, not the relevance of the enquiry which naturally occurs as to the origin of the thievish god and his relationship with the planet that bears his name. This would leave untouched the question of how such words as consider, jovial, Saturnine, Martial, Mercurial, contemplate, desire, ill-starred, desideratum, lunatic, lunes, moon-struck, moony and others have found their way into Shakespeare's plenteous vocabulary, or how the days of the week, Sun-day, Moon-day, Mar-di, Mercre-di, Thor or Jupiter's day, Freia or Venus' day and Saturn or Satur's day had their meaning for him if their astrological parentage be set aside. As for the Moon's day, his references to it are too numerous for quotation. "Midsummer Night's Dream" is extended over a period of four nights in order to satisfy the duke concerning it. The play opens with a statement of his views :—

"*Theseus.* Now, Fair Hippolyta our nuptial hour draws
on apace. Four happy days bring in another
moon.

Hippol.   Four days will quickly dream away the time
and then the moon, like a silver bow new bent
heaven, shall behold the night of our solemni-
ties."

At a later time Hermia is told to "take time to pause, and,
by the next new moon, the sealing day betwixt my love and
me, prepare to wed Demetrius", which, if it does not establish
the writer's own conviction that there is, in Solomon's words, a
time for everything, at least completes the case for his Duke of
Athens.

Interesting it is to note throughout this play, as well as
that of the "Tempest", how well the poet knew when to have
done with Zodiacs and Right Ascensions, how he subdues his
science, so prominent at other times, and allows the stars to play
their part as an attractive background to his picture.   Apos-
trophes such as those of Oberon to the planet Venus are common ;
the witchery of night is ever present ; when the stars are in
view they fulfil all that is needed of them ; anything that would
divert attention from their beauty is carefully withheld.   Only
once in the "Tempest", in Act 1, Sc. 2, does Prospero allow
the tools with which he works to show themselves :—

"I find" he says, "my Zenith doth depend upon a most
auspicious star, whose influence, if now I court not,
but omit, my fortunes will ever after droop."

This at once suggests the inner meaning of "there is a tide
in the affairs of men ;" but Prospero is Ariel's master (the im-
pulsive Ariel, born under Aries) and, as such, is supreme in
forces which lie beyond the critic's pale ; he is magician as well
as student of Astrology, and so is in the convenient position of
being able to do precisely as he wills.

In Act 1, Sc. 2, of "Winter's Tale" Polixenes speaks of
"nine changes of the watery moon" which had transpired since
he left his throne ; Leontes, in the same scene, makes a charac-
istic allusion to a planet, the nature of which he no doubt
understood for he himself was subject to it ; and, later, Camillo
says, at a crisis in his life :—

"Happy star, reign now ; here comes Bohemia."

Hermione complains, in the third scene of the second act,
that "some ill planet reigns", and, in the third act speaks of
her infant, "starred unluckily" and from her "breast haled out
to murder;" as for the Oracle business in Act 3, it is known, if

not always respected, by every student of Astrology ; though here again the artist hand is strong ; the Oracle is not loquacious, he is carefully non-committal, he does not interrupt the action by provoking wonder as to how he got his mysterious information.

If Malone was justified in maintaining that Shakespeare did not write the first part of "Henry VI" and that too especially on account of allusions therein contained, it is noteworthy that the planetary references were not included. They were probably common to all writing at the time. Bedford begins at the very outset :—

> "Hung be the heavens with black, yield day to night,
> Comets, importing change of times and states,
> Brandish your crystal tresses in the sky,
> And with them scourge the bad, revolting stars
> That have consented unto Henry's death."

Shortly afterwards he invokes the spirit of the king to "combat with adverse planets in the heavens" (compare "the stars in their courses fought against Sisera"), his whole attitude in the scene being an impressive one in this respect. The second scene affords an opportunity to note the progress made by Astronomy since Shakespeare's time ; though it may be doubted whether even now we have all the information possessed by the ancient Egyptians and Chaldeans; Joseph's reading of Pharoah's dream, for instance, being evidently based on the movements of Uranus, which we regard as discovered little more than a century ago. "Mars" says Charles, "his true moving, even as in the heavens, so in the earth, to this day is not known. Late did he shine upon the English side ; now we are victors, upon us he smiles." That is to say, we are not certain either as to his precise movement in the heavens or to the effect he has upon the earth.

Act IV., Sc. 5 of the same play introduces further evidence of the care with which the author (or his imitator) worked out such matters to their logical conclusion. Talbot cries to his son :—"I did send for thee to tutor thee ; but, oh malignant and ill-boding stars, now thou art come to the feast of death, a terrible and unavoided danger." The commentators read this as meaning unavoidable ; but unavoided is clearly meant ; that is, astrologically speaking, a danger to which you are liable and which you have made no effort to avoid. Talbot speaks as if suddenly impressed by a planetary call to aid his son ; but the aspect was not strong enough to be of service. The lad refuses to be moved ; the father thereupon sees the inevitable and concludes by saying :—"Then here I take my leave of thee fair son, born to eclipse thy life this afternoon; come, side by side together." The astro-logical crisis occurs in the seventh scene.

Julia, in Act 2, Sc. 7 of the "Two Gentlemen of Verona," says that "truer stars did govern Proteus' breath", and, in the "Merry Wives" is recorded, in reply to an Arien outburst on the part of Pym, Pistol's conviction that he is "the very Mars of malcontents." Mars, it will be remembered, is the ruler of the Zodiacal sign of Aries.

In the third scene of the opening Act of "Much Ado" we have Don John saying :—

> "I wonder that thou, being (as thou say'st thou
> art) born under Saturn, goest about to apply a
> moral medicine to a mortifying mischief."

Don John, himself an ill-aspected Saturn man, naturally objected to his ruling planet being accused of harbouring good intentions, even though of fruitless kind. To recur, however, to Mars, there is in "All 's Well" some entertaining treatment, Helena showing herself to be quite a skilled practitioner. In Act 1, Sc. 1, she says ;—"It were all one that I should love a bright particular star and think to wed it", the fuller meaning appearing later when she speaks of we "the poorer born, whose baser stars do shut us up in wishes", while at the close of the scene, there is the following :—

> *"Hel.* Monsieur Parolles, you were born under a charitable
>   star.
> *Par.* Under Mars I.
> *Hel.* I especially think under Mars.
> *Par.* Why under Mars?
> *Hel.* The wars have so kept you under that you must
>   needs be born under Mars.
> *Par.* When he was predominant ?
> *Hel.* When he was retrograde, I think, rather."

This entire Act being one of its author's most attractive Court studies, which in "Hamlet" came to such perfection, Helena's charitable construction of Mars is more readily accepted. He is here found in full knowledge of the importance of the retrogression of a planet, which might be suggested as having been in his mind when he causes the King in "Hamlet" to say :—"It is most retrograde to our desire." The retrogression of a planet was and is understood to be oppressive in effect.

In "Timon of Athens" and "As you like it" little use is made of this material, for obvious artistic reasons ; the love story would have lost romance, the tragedy would have failed in its appeal. On the other hand there are numerous allusions in "Love's Labor Lost," in particular to the influence of the moon, while purely astronomical talk is very frequent, such as that of the Bear being "over the new chimney and yet our horse is not yet packed," (time is flying, in other words) which appears in Act 2, Sc. 1 of "Henry IV." The Bastard cries despairingly in "King John," (Act 5, Sc. 6) :—"Now you stars that move in your right spheres, where be your powers?" In "Richard II." (Act 3, Sc. 4) and in the "Taming of the Shrew" (Act 4, Sc. 5) there are also exclamations similar in kind.

In the great classic play the Sooth or Truth Sayer warns Cæsar to "beware the Ides of March" and is represented throughout as being a personage who influenced his hearers, the higher class of them especially. In the opening of Act 3 the "sectary astronomical" appears again, when Cæsar says :—

"But I am constant as the Northern star, of whose true
and lasting quality there is no fellow in the firmament;"
talk of the day, no doubt, but with the weight of astronomy behind it. Nor is he neglectful of its possibilities in other ways ; like his own William, he has "a pretty wit" at times, though it be caviare to the general ; witness "Saturn and Venus" in Act 2, Sc. 4 of the second part of "Henry IV." when Hal and Poins enter from behind. To add to this there is the passage in Act 2 of "Troilus:"—

"And fly like chidden Mercury from
Jove, or like a star disorb'd ;"
which shows that years of study had made the author so familiar with the properties of the conjunctions that he could toy with them correctly, had taught him also the relative speed of planets and the importance of the orbs ; that is, the radius in which a planet is effective, as to which there are still discussions to be heard.

To the casual reader such quotations, shorn of the context and clubbed together in one collection, may appear of little moment; but, even as they are, the deduction is unavoidable that devotion to a science is necessary before it can be handled with such genial freedom and at the same time never failing relevance and accuracy.

Dryden well said that Shakespeare is often flat and even insipid, that his comic wit is frequently of the poorest, and his serious swelling degenerates sometimes into bombast ; but, he finely added "he is always great when some great occasion is presented to him ; no man can say he ever had a fit subject and did not rise to meet it." We have only to recall the knocking at the gate in "Macbeth," the hot air of the Verona streets in "Romeo," the instant arrestment of attention by the opening scene in "Hamlet," Othello's last words and Cassio's comment on them, to be once again impressed by the truth of this. Yet in nothing was he greater than in his control of means ; there can be little doubt that planetary influence was something more to him than literary garnish, yet it is never used with faddishness, never when it can be said to be out of place and disturbing to the tenor of the scene. With the exception of the significant foreboding at the end of Act 1, Sc. 4 there is no word of it in "Romeo and Juliet" until the tragic crescendo commences and the lover hears the news of Juliet's death. There the unerring dramatist strikes a chord :—

"Is it even so?" says Romeo ; "then I defy you, stars."

Still the climax is yet to come and his words, later, in the tomb :—"Here will I set up my everlasting rest and shake the yoke of inauspicious stars from this world-wearied flesh," prepares us for the end. If the writers of today had even a glimmering of such instinct for the dramatic, we might leave our theatres with less of melancholy than we do.

The final scene in "Othello" gives a similar illustration :—
"It is the cause, it is the cause, my soul. Let me not name it to you, ye chaste stars. * * * Oh heavy hour, methinks it should be now a huge eclipse of sun and moon ; but, oh vain boast, who can control his fate? Be not afraid, here is our journey's end. Oh, ill-starr'd wench."

Strongest, perhaps, is the poetic expression of his deduction from it all, in the sonnets, particularly the 14th, 15th, 25th, and 29th, of which the second in order is quoted in conclusion :–

"When I consider everything that grows,
Holds in perfection but a little moment,
That this huge state presenteth naught but shows,

Whereon the stars in secret influence comment,
When I perceive that men as plants increase,
Cheered and checked even by the selfsame sky,
Vaunt in their youthful sap, at height increase,
And wear their brave state out of memory,
Then the conceit of this inconstant stay,
Sets you most rich in youth before my sight,
And, all in war with time for love of you,
As he takes from you, I engraft you new.''

Printed in the United States
70398LV00003B/218